Praising the Paradox

PRAISING THE PARADOX

POEMS

Tina Schumann

Red Hen Press | *Pasadena, CA*

Book design by Mark E. Cull

Library of Congress Cataloging-in-Publication Data

Names: Schumann, Tina, author.
Title: Praising the paradox : poems / Tina Schumann.
Description: First edition. | Pasadena, CA : Red Hen Press, [2019]
Identifiers: LCCN 2018043562 | ISBN 9781597096171
Classification: LCC PS3619.C4818 A6 2019 | DDC 811/.6—dc23
LC record available at https://lccn.loc.gov/2018043562

The National Endowment for the Arts, the Los Angeles County Arts Commission,
the Ahmanson Foundation, the Dwight Stuart Youth Fund, the Max Factor Family
Foundation, the Pasadena Tournament of Roses Foundation, the Pasadena Arts
& Culture Commission and the City of Pasadena Cultural Affairs Division, the
City of Los Angeles Department of Cultural Affairs, the Audrey & Sydney Irmas
Charitable Foundation, the Kinder Morgan Foundation, the Allergan Foundation,
the Meta & George Rosenberg Foundation, and the Riordan Foundation partially
support Red Hen Press.

First Edition
Published by Red Hen Press
www.redhen.org

ACKNOWLEDGMENTS

The author wishes to thank the journals and anthologies in which the following poems appeared.

American Poetry Journal: "Calculations" and "Friday"; *American Society: What Poets See*: "A Day in the Life" and "A World of Want"; *Ascent*: "For I Have Sinned"; *Atticus Review*: "Consider This"; *Augurybooks.com*: "Wednesday"; *Bracken Magazine*: "A Flurry of Finches"; *Crab Creek Review*: "After," "Banishment at Noon" and "Random Winter Day"; *Cranky Literary Journal*: "This is My Confessional"; *Cimarron Review*: "Traveling Instructions" and "You Are Here"; *Generations Literary Journal*: "Momentary Mother"; *Harpur Palate*: "Autumn"; *Nimrod*: "Ode to Time, Lance and December Rain" and "Overture (*anticipation*) . . ."; *Oracle Fine Arts Review*: "Ocean Fugue"; *Palabra*: "In Oaxaca"; *Parabola*: "Vanishing Point"; *Poemeleon*: "Sunday"; *Poetry and Place Anthology*: "Stoplight Outside Hamburger Harry's, 2:00 am" (reprint); *The Midwest Quarterly*: "Not Dead, But Lost" and "Highway 99"; *Raven Chronicles*: "In Oaxaca" (reprint); *San Pedro River Review*: "Stoplight Outside Hamburger Harry's, 2:00 am"; *Skagit River Poetry Festival Anthology 2014*: "Praising the Paradox"; *subTerrain*: "It's Like This" and "Neither Here nor There"; *The American Journal of Poetry*: "Rehab Fugue #1"; *Terrain.org*: "Another Sunday," "A Seasonal Accord," "Home Redux" and "Winter/Affirmation"; *The Human*: "Another Voyage"; *The Lost River Review*: "Central Ave." and "It is the Night"; *Verse Daily*: "Repository."

Gratitude to the following mentors, friends and cohorts who helped in so many ways with the creation of these poems. Linda Bierds, Sharon Bryan, Kevin Clark, Stephen Corey, Danika Dinsmore, Casey Fuller, Lola Haskins, Christine Hemp, Judith Kitchen, Erin Coughlin Hollowell, Jill McCabe Johnson, Jill McGrath, Dorianne Laux, Linda Malnack, Gerry McFarland, Lia Purpura, Sherry Reniker, Stan Rubin, Sheryl Sirotnik, Nancy Weeks and the Rainier Writers Workshop at Pacific Lutheran University.

CONTENTS

I

a subtitle of self. . . .

II

no less subject to the elements . . .

III

negotiating fault lines . . .

Praising the Paradox

I don't believe in God, but I miss Him.
—Julian Barnes

I

a subtitle of self. . . .

Traveling Instructions

Because I am feeling like a house today—
all brackets and blueprints—you must appeal to the dog
in me; the one whose snout travels the floor
for any known scent, any signifier of home.
Over the dust that has settled into each mitered joint.
Past the oak molding sanded to a fine point.
I do not tarry for I do not doubt—I simply turn left
when turning left is called for. Because the sidewalk
that buckles at the threshold to the house
covers the roots of trees that meander under walkway
and grass, twine the pipes and reach for the light
of the backyard's cool, you must appeal to the weed in me;
the one whose roots run deep, whose face is neither fair
nor friendly, but simply there. Because I did not know
what I did not know—I traveled
between desire and compulsion, yen and need, plan and arrival.
I did not query for I could not answer, I simply left
blank spaces along the way; an ellipse here, a dash there.
The ground, now soaked
with weeks of constant rain gave way
beneath my leathered soles. I did not stop
to think twice, the earth is the earth after-all,
taken to burdening itself with all aspects
of nature's wild ways.
Because the dress I was forced to wear that Easter
I was three was scratchy and poufy and far too yellow
you must appeal to the child in me; the one that ran
towards my father holding the camera and yearned
to yell *I hate this dress*, but words of protest had not come

to me yet. No matter. That is all in the backwaters
of memory, so you must appeal to the river
in me; all bend and flow, brush and bramble, taproot and rock.

CALCULATIONS

No matter what you start out with
you always end up with so much less.
—*The Hours*

Myself—
the abridged, the novel that never was, sub-
tracted, abbreviated, a subtitle of self.
        So soon to be
the slightest signal of a women, draped in my tattered flag,
holding a box of zeroes
        and a mouthful of air.
When the end comes it won't matter.
        In between
I will have thought myself large, whole, my travels far,
experiences grand, many stories to tell and so on . . . .
But what emancipation—
        to *be* diminished, reduced
to the absolute; a room deprived
of its contents, melting ice
at the bottom of someone's glass,
the tipped bottle and its residual remains.
        What delicious deliverance,
what radiant resignation
to be so much
less than I
could have ever hoped for.

You Are Here

And the day is full
of fallacy (pathetic and otherwise) and thus
were my hours of magical thinking spent
within a demarcation of days and the cockatiel remained
poised in her wire cage hung from the apricot tree
and inside the razors remained
sharp and the lilies did lie and all was quiet
except for the rain as it hit the metal roof
and I did lose faith in myself and was angry
about that and the curtains did hang and crease
and the jackets pegged on silver hooks waited
to be put on and the shoes were silent and the walls
did not move as I thought of my state never to know
who I was only some vague inclination of person-
hood neither daughter nor wife nor friend nor sister
goodbye to all that and the berries did droop under the weight
of yesterday's rain and the trousers hung on hangers and the shirts
held their form and my breath rose and fell and my fibula remained
solid blood warm and flowing and my heart in its grave
cavern of consistency kept up its rhythmic hum—I am this
machine—a body—thou art always with me
thy skin and thy cartilage they comfort me
even now—in October—waiting for someone
to choose me for the eternal game of dodge ball
—a tip of the hat, a nod from the bartender a wink
from the waitress—oh ego how I do cleave to thee
thy sermons and thy cravings they comfort me
and I shall dwell in the maze forever.

ANOTHER SUNDAY

And the eggs have been broken.
The bacon laid to rest. The belly of the dishwasher satisfied
at last. Oh, satiated coffeed world with your mind

in reverse and your soft body bound in flannel sheets,
how have I come to you again?
In the crash of weekday waves breaking

on the splintered porch, in the gravity and weightlessness
that hefts this ball of earth, its rotation part ritual,
part benediction. How I covet the hours

we will spend in the endless hedge grove
of banal and quiet tasks; picking up the magazines,
shaking out the doorstep's mat.

In the yellow state I am in I cannot divine the day
or fathom a future form. From here it's nothing
more than alliteration of motion. Though the calendar

pinned to the kitchen wall gapes in silent notation,
all attempts at formulation remain null.
Tomorrow I will don my grease-coat of complaint,

my lab-wear of ego. I will stand in the doorway
and admire the way the shore so soon becomes
the ocean floor.

Random Winter Day

All afternoon we have been waiting
for snow the weatherman promised
at noon. Unreliable though he is
we plied the pantry with potatoes and bread,
milk, and a chicken crouched in the freezer.
Now there is time for reverie
to take up larger swaths of the mind. Time
to survey the rooms, walk the floors,
confuse memory with memento, artifact
with fact—like a portrait
of some long dead family uncovered
in the attic; as silent as the grave, as unknowable
as the remnants scattered in their wake.
The man has perched a bowler on his knee, the rim
of the women's petticoat frames the buttons
on a turned-out shoe. What particulars
quantify them now? Here—in suburbia—
among the old houses made new, the mouth
of every garage tight-lipped, the amorphous
whistle from the train tracks and the occasional car
that guns it up the street. I've written this poem before;
the little soul encapsulated in her little hut.
I am learning to live again
with unstable elements; the ghostly motion
of a garden swing, the distant whirr
of wheels and engine, an ambulance blaring
across the valley floor. Here, in the pre-snow silence,
there is time to let slip the juxtaposition of now

and then, house and street, portrait and memory.
Nothing but time to wait
for the texture of twilight to appear
on the kitchen wall, a flutter of white
to float across the face of a window. Now
I will silence the radio, pull out the knife
by its tail and prepare to cleave flesh
from bone, question from action,
time from the stillness of relics.

AUTUMN

You know how the world comes at you like that?
You're driving down some tree-lined street
with Vivaldi or Corelli
lilting their way from the radio.
The sun is casting prisms on the leaves,
the leaves easy in their fall.
All questions have quieted.
You are convinced that even the asphalt is happy
to be what it is: solid, stoic, the backbone of a day.
Up ahead the next three lights are green,
and you are passing the school yard at St. Paul's,
where all the kids in their blue and green uniforms
are bright angels, bearers of light.
There goes Stone Way Cleaners where they are steaming and pressing,
steaming and pressing just for you. The world is stuck
on go, proceed, *avanti*. No one could imagine
how enlightened you've become
in the cabin of your car, clarity at the wheel,
on the rim of tears, with your velocity of awe,
your rapid rolling toward some small truth—on and on like that.

A World of Want

You think your life will go on
like this forever—weekly trips
to the garbage bin, untangling
the green snake of hose between the ferns
and the delphiniums, the coral bells
leaning their long necks
against the back fence.
Today, as I watched the carousel
of cars turn one by one through
the intersection and onto the freeway
I tried to imagine each life.
Not so much where they were
going, but what they were made of:
wounds, illusions, desires, deceits. . . .
Through all of this a preoccupation
with the next perceived need floats-up
like thought bubbles inside my head:
Coffee, Cheetos, sex, a new blouse, a larger house,
a desk fan, appreciation from that one specific person,
the phones chirp, the trip to France.
If I could quiet this conga-line of cravings
what lingering longings would I lament?
What radiant unattached insights
would I muster? Who would I be
without my constant yearnings?
It's a *world* of want. You get the idea.

For I Have Sinned

It has been five hundred days,
countless meals and many mountain tops
since my last confession.
            I have lusted in my heart
for the woman who sells me my morning coffee.
It's just the way she stands sometimes
with her back to me and her waist turned just so.
I'd like to take her cheek into the bed of my palm,
tell her what a gift she is; she of the tender smile,
she of the warm offerings. I have coveted
my neighbor's garden. I love it
and I don't love it. The symmetry of it all.
The telltale heap of compost that mocks me
from the parking strip, every Tube Rose
preening in the sun, the Gerbera Daisies bobbing
on their brainless stems, and the way she idles at the edge
of beds in her drab green Wellingtons. The serious planning
of grace written all over her face.
            Gluttony can't be helped.
We've been over this, we've covered my inability
to just say no. Like when I packed my suitcases
full of Balsamico and Grappa, what I didn't tell you
is that for days before I had eaten truffles
at every meal. I let their heady fungalness permeate.
I let each white sliver melt
on my tongue like the body of Christ.
            And there are hours of sloth
like baptisms of guilt. Submerge me,
cover me I say I am a sucker

for the easy move, the natural incline,
any tripping toward entropy.

        It's no use. I know what you'll prescribe.
I found nine Rosaries in my mother's bedroom
after she died. Look at her *now*.
What a set-up; this propensity toward failings.
Lord, thy name is entrapment.
Let's get on with it.
For God's sake—
Bless me.

BANISHMENT AT NOON

From where I sit on the campus steps
I see the twin steeples
   of the cathedral four blocks uptown
rise in relief against a pale tint of sky.
The roofs of small houses kowtow at its side.
   A slant of sunlight
      and wave of trees
   all conspire to design
a watercolor portrait—a sudden village.
   Still. Impenetrable.

Students make their way from fields and doorways,
their shadows long and quick
      against the brick.
I am in love with their disregard, their many ways
   of unknowing.
Sitting on the steps of this Jesuit school I try to write
   poetry but can't
keep my eyes off that damned church,
   the sky, the clouds,
the jab and flow of that girl's cotton skirt
   making more of this material world
than either of us
      will ever know.

Praising the Paradox

Except for the raging cherry blossom

across the street

    the neighborhood is quiet,

only the orange cat and I

      survey the scene.

Walking this way, along the landscape's edge,

my own mythology spills out

    before me

in the slow staccato of a day. Whatever

I take in I am soon to name:

      sage, gate, grass, pathway

to the open lawn.

    From the pea vines to the dandelions

I am making it up as I go along.

    Each step

a worn declaration; *Be here, love this.*

Under the Hosta's broad leaves

there are always disappointing secrets;

a snail's abandoned shell, a start of ivy

from the neighbor's yard, small tufts

of chickweed

in the shaded green.

Though easy to pull

this weed

spreads fast,

its soft roots breaking

like bundles of loose thread, its union

with the soil

tenuous at best. Hard won.

Here I am again—

praising the paradox.

What was I thinking? Nature owes me

nothing.

I come here for the facts

and facts are what I get—

from the curled edge of every blown leaf

to the brittle stance

of every downward facing stalk.

WINTER/AFFIRMATION

Outside—
the peonies are beyond their deaths.
But in here—on our continent of a bed—
we are busy showing each other pictures
of ourselves: mouth to rib, back to belly, palm
to hip. Here is the reciprocal breath, the sanctified
taking—my only chance
at reformation.
All day long I live in my head
and as the house bends toward twilight
you say, *Listen, you've got it all wrong.*
Lie down. Get a load of our quiet profiles.
Outside—
the tubers have turned inward,
away from the light.
But in here—in our cathedral of a room—
we are busy ridding ourselves
of words, holding our faces
to the mirror. Carrying out
our best directive.

VANISHING POINT

How am I a self
when I am
constantly disappearing?

A traveling venue
of water
and sinew—

I am a story
I made up
in my head . . .

looks good in hats,
won't eat oysters,
fears infirmity.

Touch me. I am fluid.

In all my transparency
my body is
betraying me

just as
the plot
demanded.

I would deny this
distant progression
of time and cells

if the mirror
were not
such a talker.

Kiss me. I am corruptible.

So what
are we
made of?

Stories—
Just when you think
you could not take

one more
here comes another.
You keep right on

living—
piling up
your stories

like cordwood
and the lying-self
keeps pace

with daily duties;
meals to prepare,
pills to take.

How could you
keep on if you did not
deny your vanishing point?

Look at me. I won't last long.

November

Hardened ground. Grass almost black

    and still

the question remains—do I repeat myself? Not only in this life,

    but the next?

The house issues its usual sighs. Crows pick the ash tree bare,

    perched like finials in frozen air.

Fated sky, itinerant world, what will I unlearn

    that I take as gospel now?

Watery mirage of neighbor's hemlock wavers

    through the old pane—living

    on the other side. Every day

it's a snap, it's a shrug and suddenly I am

    amid

another season. A Bedouin

        bent on place.

                Unbidden.

        Ready to capitulate.

September

Early evening, late summer

    barbeques, cosmos on the deck. Voices

from the neighborhood drift through an open window.

Someone is telling a joke. Someone is waiting

    for a punch line.

Burst of laughter, clink of glasses, and I—

the uninvited guest—a party

    to artifice.

        Nevertheless,

there it is; the perfect invention

    of a life not lived.   I recall

the tour tape at Alcatraz, an ex-prisoner's voice told of New Year's Eve—

    lights out, lying in his bunk,

        he could hear the revelry

from the city piers, the pop of Champagne, the diminished chord

of women's voices, faint music from the bandstand

blown in on the breeze.

A Seasonal Accord

Nettles grow tall just behind the backyard fence,
out of reach—all season—growing on the sneak.
I hear them scuff and sway across the wood.
I haven't the heart to cut them dead.

It happens every year,
the same tacit alliance—
the same wordless exchange
of life, death and resurrection.

I peruse catalogs of false potential,
eye the seductive carnage-to-be.
Each page more raging
with chi than the one before.

Digging at the roots,
turning under cover crops,
I bend to the bed, rotate and plow.
Play at the putting off—

the inevitable prize of rot.
Though every adolescent sprout is pleasant,
congenial, a charmer full of fibs
and propaganda, I can't help but ask;

When does the real work begin?
When does the sky give leave
and let reason fall to the ground?
Why can't I just say it?

I do it for the loss, the fragility,
the decay so achingly sought
and the bloom never as satisfying
as the falling away.

FALL/REPRISE

Waiting for the light to turn
green I watch evening descend
on the park; a scarlet rise of sky
behind a stand of alders.

At the corner, a mother waits in tweed jacket
and brown tights, her carriage held before her.
The baby under a blanket of lumberjack plaid.
Piano chords from a nearby window

guide leaves to the ground. In that instant
I thought my innocence had returned—
or maybe faith. But faith in what? Time?
Seasons? The blind consistency of nature?

I held the notion for only a moment
and hoped the song would not change
the mottled sky, the mother, the child, the trees—
all on their way. It is not tragedy

that compels such thoughts, but routine,
comfort—like holding your own hand,
the momentary glimpse held still . . . by light,
by song, by the tenuous fall.

Sunday

And 4:00 a.m.
is full of 4:00 a.m.
I ought to sleep, but instead ponder
the mandate *collect yourself.*
What does it mean
to reclaim bits of oneself?
The eyeball that rolled towards the radiator,
a crest of hair flouncing near the door jam, thoughts
plastered on the wainscoting like so much paper.
Should I arrange them on the windowsill
for further observation? Show them off
to other collectors? Later, these bits will appear
to move as one; a functioning assemblage
of well-oiled parts—it will grind
coffee beans, take down the mugs and make
nice with the toaster. The part called the mouth will holler
your eggs are ready. It will,
in unison, pause, blink, sigh,
put on some Brubeck and take to couch
with The Times. I can see it now
reclining against the red pillows,
moving the cat from lap to carpet
while the bit called *the brain* or *psyche* thinks
about accomplishing something meaningful,
and soon feels guilty for not accomplishing something
meaningful. Later it will pay homage
to our lady of swirling laundry, search for signs of life
with the remote control, hope

the vacuum will redeem it.
It will, as usual, realize that dinner is a given
and peruse old recipes, drink red wine,
—anticipate a shrouded Monday.
And all the while this is what the sign above the door will say;
Survey. Repent. Collect yourself.

II

no less subject to the elements . . .

CONSIDER THIS

Time may be an abstraction, but it makes the days go by.
—John Koethe

Imagine, if you will, that I were not
          an acolyte
among the living,
          my days more than a catechism
of routine. From the nasturtiums
floating face-up
          in their glass bowl
to the window I shattered
          that summer I was broke. I go on
exhausting years
          on the unknowable.

Consider how easy it is to look up
          from your half-eaten
breakfast with its drying riverbed of yoke
          and compromised toast
              to stare out
at the interstate as if in prayer.
          The waitress transfixed
          as well, her
coffee-pot suspended
          in mid-air . . . *we interrupt this*
American morning to bring you
          a moment of desperate
reflection.

And every day laying down
        little pronouncements.
Examining the artifice
        of life like some multi-faceted gem;
not beautiful exactly, but curious. Foreign
        in the way delusion is strange
and familiar at the same time—an alien
        notion setting up
a homestead in the mind.
        Harbinger
of the great ego crash to come.

In spite of judgments
        skidding across
                my thoughts like hard rain.
In spite of my heart
        clattering its tin cup
along the bars of its cage.
        It's one articulation
after another.

Consider that which leaves
        one empty—devoid
             of any fullness
that might have mattered
        in its time?
Jarring insights, illumination

that washes over you
like cold water—and then . . .
a trip to the dump, the aching
     overhead lights
of a drugstore, a void
     where your mother's voice used to be.

Highway 99

September 2nd and already the air has turned

      to chill. The tops of the neighbor's bamboo trees

           sway and dip

their leafy heads away and towards

         each other—agreeing and disagreeing—

reminding me of the billowy

      human-like balloons

erected at car dealerships

      and one-day-blow-out-sales—faceless, limp

arms gesturing in futile attempts at flight.

         The elongated head dipping dangerously

      close to the ground

until forced air keels the figure up and proud again

         for one heroic moment, only to collapse

      back on itself—wasted, defeated—sad

giant staggerings, a waft of puppeteering.

Its quasi-human form an implication

to do what? Surrender your will? Give up now

and admit you are so much air

blown into a casing?

No less subject to the elements, no more swelling with hope

than the next enigmatic object.

You recognize the impulse—you've battled the burden

to remain

erect daily, quelled the desire to be

on the ground, flat-out, done in.

You've known for a while now—no matter how bright the sun

casts its face towards the shops and cars, how lovely the girls

appear in their summer dresses or how clear as light

the boys at the bus stop—it's all amplitude

and impermanence—faltering in stages

like some fluttering icon

of intermittent optimism—flagging you down

along Highway 99.

STOPLIGHT OUTSIDE
HAMBURGER HARRY'S, 2:00 A.M.

See the dark traffic of morning
disperse, the windshield blurred by rain
and the rhythmic tick of a turn signal.
See the bartender wipe down his bar
as if he were circling the moon's orbit.
The neon *open* sign in the window reflecting
blue and red against the pallor of his face.
See the television flicker a movies end
and the waitress nod her goodbye—
         no words between them now.
After years of repetition, this is the silence
they have come to. From Monday night's
football crowd to the middle-aged couple
who treat themselves every Thursday.
Reduced to the stripped down
directives of *two Coronas* and *order up*—
What more would they say?
Their thoughts come on
like the hot slap of meat on metal
and just as quickly fade. No words now,
only the slow exhale of another night's routine,
the pull of a chain to quiet lights, the rattle of keys
to bolt out the sun.

ANOTHER VOYAGE

*– MILAN 12/4/02 (Reuters) – The remains of an Italian man who packed his
bags 44 years ago and told friends he was leaving for America were found inside
one of the walls of his former home. Inside a thick wall in the cellar was found
human remains, two packed suitcases, a trowel and other equipment to make a
wall, a rusted rifle and a bottle with a suicide note. The note, headed with the
name Nemo Cianelli, explained that the man had discovered he had an incurable
disease and had decided to kill himself. He said he had invented the tale of going to
America to avoid upsetting his family.*

If death is a country, a new world
of plaster and beams, then it is a land
of anonymous travelers. Its maps concise.
Legends full of stop signs and cellar doors.

If, after long use the body becomes a measurable object,
a thing that must be concealed, then it is a vessel
loaded for bear. Who knows what you'll need
in that new Canaan.

If we are anything we are builders.
Forever calling in reinforcements,
buttressing our way to safety.
Fortification becomes our forte.

If, in the landscape called the end
we can look at those that remain,
those still unconcerned with brackets
and the bearing of weight—

If, we can look at them and lie
like there's no tomorrow, then it can be said
that the Hudson overflows with forgiveness,
the ships never as buoyant with possibility.

If, with the final news we become
more lucent than the living, more radiant
and steady, then I'll welcome the
foremen in me. I'll study the structure

of houses, scaffolding
schematics and footprints.
The soft spread of mortar to brick.
The architecture of forever.

PRELUDE, ANAHEIM HILTON

Staring out the window of my rented room
I am on hold with the bank
when over the muffled din
of Musak I realize there is no place

on earth less amenable to poetry
than the Anaheim Hilton.
The nameless instruments
intended to sooth

remind me of nothing. They are allies
to the mirage of heat radiating
off the asphalt and irrigated turf.
Cartoons in place of an orchard.

The canvas constructed stalls
in the flea market across the street
waver in the hot wind—old men
are selling toys and tires of unknown origin.

Screams from the white kids
in the hotel pool rise over screams
from the Mexican kids in the dusty parking lot.
I'm getting out. I'm hanging up.

One last shuttle ride to the happiest place
on earth. One last thigh-to-thigh
bounce-bounce with sweaty strangers
and their deflated, day-after-Christmas kids.

One last glance
at the driver's lined forehead
in the rearview mirror.

A Variant Phase

See this avatar take on the day;
that well-dressed agent
on my behalf.

See how she moves
between the backdoor
and the garden gate.

Joints engage, limbs propel
her in a forward motion. See
how she . . . carries on.

She's smooth she is,
that one enrobed
in the other.

The one who shows
you this, but not that.
A sleight of hand,

a trick with light, a bit
of familiar smoke screen.
If I could embody her,

minus the division— oh, what a fullness
there would be.

It would not take
some ambitious God
to create her every day.

This incarnation of robotic
proportions. See her waver
at the changing light,

so soon inside the evening
door materializes a woman
of other means.

AUBADE WITH GREY ROBE

5:00 a.m. and I am waiting for the slap
of your feet on the kitchen linoleum.
A shuffle of papers while you look
for the sports page.

The cat door clicks into place
while the neighbor's truck chokes
in the alley. I imagine you've fallen
in the bathroom, numb and silent,

thinking of me.
Or perhaps the basement door was left
unlocked—an intruder has shot you
and is now headed for the bedroom.

What would I do without you?
Never love again?
Lose ten pounds, cut my hair
and move to Vermont?

It seems I ask for these moments
of terror. The spiral into the possible
headline: *Husband Found Dead
While Wife Sleeps.*

Now the door opens softly, casting
its long shadow across the bed,
you move slowly so as not to wake me.
The grey robe rolls off your shoulders

as it has a thousand times before
and I see how this one motion
is proof; you are whole, here
by chance or choice.

Neither Here nor There

I coaxed you
into a walk.
You indulged me
this time.

Hand in hand down our street
we pass a row of cherry blossoms
in full regalia. Rice-paper petals
carpet asphalt and gutter.
Biblical-beams of sunlight
shaft through the open clouds.

I am easily bamboozled
by such mid-spring insanity;
the solar gift of a 2:00 p.m. stroll,
your skin on mine—
I was about to state the obvious.
I was about to say *how beautiful.*

When I saw your narrowed eyes
scan from treetop to street,
street to branch. You shook
your head slowly
and said
what a mess.

THIS IS MY CONFESSIONAL

This house, with furniture
that does not comfort.
Like pliable steel, it tries.
How stupid to lose sleep
over this. If I am not here,
then I am longing for here.
The faucet that drips
a reminder, the frozen poplar
stump out back.
Forgive yourself—he said.
You are not to blame
for the deconstruction
of stars, objects and their affinities,
your lack of a Paterson.
Home is where your head belong.
Oh, the *characters*
you make up. Awfully creative
in your dreams little girl.
And aren't you always the little girl?
Never the one to change
a tire, never the confident mother,
    piano player, or smoker.
No, you like to eat, turn up the heat,
smell the same man, walk nowhere
on your treadmill. Come down
from your cliff dwelling.
Be a rat.

IT IS THE NIGHT

That lets me down.
When the house seems unknown,
the body next to me unreachable.
Some sinister recess has commenced
and I must wait it out. Row my boat
hard against the arcing tide, keep my head,
pay the sandman twice. Welcome the night-
ly oblivion that sees me through those no-good hours
between two and four when every failure rushes in—
every folly confirmed.
Big questions slated on the bathroom wall.
Harassing every dust mote for answers; what have I done?
Or worse, what haven't I?
This stupor could have no future.
I am as flat and dumb as the kitchen floor.
As heedless as the doors.
As silent as the spoons.

NOT DEAD, BUT LOST

That's the way I see my mother now—
in my dreams—not dead, but lost.
I spot her in a crowd
at some vast open-air market. I follow her
past long rows of vendor stalls,
never quite catching up. Sometimes she appears
behind the wheel of her car
in an endless parking lot—waiting.
Or a puff of grey hair suddenly moves
among the rotating O's of clothing carousels.
I have left her in Women's Blouses,
distracted by crock pots and couches.
I can see by the expression on her face
she is more than a little annoyed—
leaving her alone all those years.
I'm sorry I say, *I didn't know . . .*
—I thought you were dead.
Well, she says, *let's go, I've been waiting*
long enough. It's time to go
home.

Ten

Because I could not get the face of the clock above the fridge
        to reveal its secrets (its needled hands pointed to nothing
more prophetic than now or later), I chose to live
        without time. Things would happen when they happened.
There were, after all, many things to be frightened of: Killer Bees
        from South American, Hell's Angels
                from Oakland, rising voices on the other side
                of the bedroom wall.
Because boys had it easy and were allowed to command
        their bodies and not the other way around, I ignored boys and chose to live
        without them for as long as I could. They were, after all, only interesting
                as men.
Because I thought that every ten-year-old lived
        with two languages swirling above her head, I ignored my mother
on the phone to her sisters, my grandmother's mid-sentence switch
        from English to Spanish,
the cacophony of conversation at every Sunday dinner. Let them speak
        the language I had no use for.
There were, after all, many ways to speak, I knew this already; a look
        shot across the dining room table, the slight turn of a body
        when passing in the hall, the way a head was held
                in the long silence of the car.
Because I was allowed to wear jeans to school only on Wednesdays,
        I ignored my mother's rule and snuck them
in my backpack, changed in the tight stall of the girl's bathroom.
        Its antiseptic floors too close for comfort.
I was, after all, not the skirt and blouse kind of girl. It did me no good.
        She found out anyway—followed me home one afternoon, confronted me
                at the screen-door, her face a shadowy patch of features.

Because, lying in bed at night the adult voices hovered like cartoon bubbles
        in the space between the ceiling and my face,
blurry and nonsensical, I ignored them and stopped trying
        to comprehend. Instead, I deemed their words
a dead language. I had, after all, become a palindrome to them,
        the same thing backward as forward.

CENTRAL AVE.

Along the avenue a regiment of trees
stood rigid, and in the house as big as a
Saturday the clocks ticked on amid stagnant air,
slack doorknobs, paint chips—

the rumble of casings and pocket doors.
Such images culled from memory
travel in a slow migration
of thought, clogging the throat with things.

From the old garage that clung to the flanks of the house
like a lesser organ to the girl who dragged a bicycle
out by its neck, past the grease pit, ice pick, wood beams
and the grass that waited for no one.

Inside the basement's underground life
remained calm: ash box, vice grip, hook
and eye; reliable occupants
biding their time.

It is not the memory of wood
to be blamed, or the dining room's
hermetic servitude where dust motes floated
like lost chromosomes.

The house and the girl kept their distance
from the adult figures who idled
in dim lit rooms, meal after meal,
words masticated like tough meat.

Perhaps their story still remains
staged among the accoutrements of desire;
Playboys, stockings, cologne, a bed
too wide to fill. Memory, as usual speaks

in the sudden recollection of things.
Small wonder the girl left
for homes less perilous
and the avenue was endless.

HOME REDUX

This morning in the garden
      the soil smelled sweet.
Something beyond root
      or loam.
Something about skin
      and the body.
Say mother
      or perfumery.
Say memory. . . .
Last night I dreamt
      of the old house again.
The rooms appeared larger,
      hallways deep and wrong angled.
No end to the floors,
      no *out there.*
Only more doors, lamps on bedside tables
      turned low, dishes draining
      on a sideboard.
Why *that* house
      when there were so many others?
That house
      where there was never remedy,
only more inquiry; unopened boxes, talk
      of paintings and rugs lost in transit—so much left
      behind.
Today the grapevines reach
      their long arms over the roof
      of *this* house
and I wonder

at memory's storerooms.
At our capacity
        to accrue
the framework of windows, attic and crawlspace.
        Because I could not work it out then
I interrogate that house again and again,
        run the tips of my fingers
over plaster and paint—like a blind person
        feeling my way
along the backs of chairs and across lampshades,
        I make my way through
the tyranny of rooms.

A Flurry of Finches

Why hadn't I noticed them before?
a flurry of finches in the ash tree
just this side of the front fence.
The week of my mother's funeral
and suddenly there they are; ten or more busy workers
in velvet suites of black and beige. Darting from branch
to limb, toothpick twigs in tiny beaks.
One or two eyed me quickly
with a sideways tilt of the head and moved on.
Why now? I've walked beneath this tree twice a day
for fifteen years and never once a finch, much less
a battalion of them.
                    Finches—her favorite.
When I was young she kept them
in white cages hung in a corner
of the kitchen. Male and females
springing nervously from plastic perch to wire frame.
When my father cleaned their cages
one small body or another would flutter
out the open door and cling to a curtain rod.
He would approach the frightened escapee
cautiously and catch it in softly cupped hands
between window and wall.
I imagined its furious minute hearts
beating against the dark enclosure of his hands.
He said they would not be afraid
            of what they could not see.

COMMUNIQUÉ

I am finally reading Anna Karenina.
You won't know this, and my need

to tell you won't change matters.
I keep thinking there must be a line to you.

Some secret number I've yet to be given.
I know life was hard.

You could be difficult.
I could be stoic.

The stronger your need, the more
I withheld. Such was our affliction.

Now, all I have is wordless faith
that some part of you understood

that you left your mark, that you remain.
Not only in the loose skin of my ageing hands

or the crack of my voice in early morning hours,
but in what you sought out: the epic, the tragic,

the inevitable crush of the powerful on the weak.
And when I finally get to Doctor Zhivago

and The Brothers Karamazov you won't know this either,
but I'll keep telling you. This will be our new story. A silent one.

In Oaxaca

After my father and I pulled ourselves up
and scaled back down the steep stairs of the pyramid,
I climbed into the naugahyde backseat of our pea-green Maverick.
A girl my age approached the window
and with a toothsome smile held her corn-husk doll
up to her cheek for me to see. The vest of her dress
crisscrossed her chest in green, yellows, orange and reds.
Her braided hair was black, her skin dark brown.
I returned her wide-eyed stare and pirouetted Barbie
by her blond hair. Our smiles soon ceased.
It was not about the dolls or the ancient ground,
but what could not be hidden
from the eye; two girls from the same hemisphere—
worlds apart. Without the awkward camouflage of age
or the deceit of language we stared deep and long.
As long as we could before the car pulled away.

OCEAN FUGUE

The memory is beginning to fade.

    The repetitive replaying has lessened. Psychic fracture

nearly healed. For many years if someone said *fear*

    that California coastline would appear.

My father's wet chest, his arms clamped tight around my six-year-old body.

    His final fed-up insistence that I stop fearing water.

I clung to his neck, screaming out in breathless bursts

    as he walked us deliberately into the ocean. His forward gaze did not falter.

He did not whisper words of reassurance or try to make me laugh.

    His clinched jaw, his silent exasperation

at my senseless dread ricocheted off the crescendo of white caps

    rolling their way toward us.

OVERTURE *(anticipation)*

When my father dies, it will happen
as it always happens; a midnight drive
across the desert, tumbleweeds
over headlights, someone's small house

adrift in the distance. His own orphaned
image receding into the horizon.
It will be as easy as reclining my head
against velvet cushions, though sharp

as the panic of falling
in a dream. And memory, that renegade
apostle, that curbside huckster selling
shadows and regret, will take his usual position

before the footlights, his back to me
as always, the black tails of his coat
draping coolly down his back, parting
with each fluid gesture.

With his baton held high,
he will cue the orchestra
and begin to slowly, slowly
tap out a two-four tempo.

Intermezzo

When it happens, it will happen
      as it always does—inevitably, like a body
in retrograde, poker face held firm, a disappearance
      in the night, a discordant departure—
little elsewheres everywhere . . .
Together we will be
      a confusion of white space—blank notes, thin
and faltering in our dissonance—a final dissention;
      always going . . . almost gone.

Overture (*resignation*)

When my father dies, it will happen
as it always does; high wind through pipes,
low fog rolling off the lake,
a dream of drowning.

Any sudden scenario
that startles then subsides.
I will be back in the ache
of it, negotiating with ghosts—

half orphan, half meteor.
Like the end of a performance
it will have nothing
and everything to do with me.

It will culminate in reverberations—
then ambient noise, the overture finally over.
There will be polite rumblings
from the audience, a scuff of heels

on concrete, the whoosh and slam
of a taxi arriving and departing.
I will straighten my scarf, like a flag
of resignation and walk home in frozen air.

Rehab Fugue #1

My father is losing his mind
and I am holding up
half the sky. Maneuvering planets
into perpetual night.

Hourly he reassigns his possessions
new homes: the phone in the suitcase,
his wallet to the sock drawer, the TV
remote asleep amongst the towels.

Months earlier, after his storm of backfires,
I stood sentry. The past and present rode out
in tandem. He became an amalgamation
of selves, refuting every synaptic misfire.

Deep in the bog
of memory, he could not tell
the physician how many children he had.
He mistook eggs for coffee, water for wine.

From his inclined bed, he recited
a lame rendition of Dem Bones;
his elbow connected to the telephone,
fingers to the wires in the wall.

In dreams, I turned his stubbled face
left then right, on a constant quest
for the angry son, fiery suitor,
the father that never was.

Eighty-two years and he still wants more.
Even the struggle will do. Another round
in the ring, the daily rope-a-dope
of life barely keeping him akimbo.

Whatever . . . release me
from numb creation. I am done
with madness and its grey
approaches.

The nurses think he's charming
and we all want to live forever.

REPOSITORY

Is this what the body finally becomes? A sentient bibliography
of record and recall; every story, event, and memory—
a conveyer of minutiae that permeates

the flesh and embodies the archives of a life—
where every gesture must be scribed
on the gray slate of bones; a scrimshaw

some lonely sailor held the point of a knife to, pausing
to blow the white powder residue out to sea and staring up
at the stars in wonder at what to tell and what to leave out.

WEDNESDAY

Today I sat at my desk,
moved a few books around.
Thought of my demise.
I wrote a letter to a friend's mother
thanking her for the Longfellow;
she'd heard I was a poet and naturally assumed.
I ate when my body said *eat*.
I drank water—cold and slick
it slipped down my throat.
I waited for the mailman
to walk up the steps. I heard his start
and stop, the lift and lowering
of the lid, the sharp turn of his boots
on dry leaves. I waited, and he came.
I listened, and he left. He and I
and the crows and the UPS man
and the kid down the street with the basketball
are all figures moved by instinct and need,
obligation, desire, and boredom. But I digress.
I picked the glass up, set the glass down,
stood up, walked the floor, looked out the window,
cursed the grass, and thought, thought, thought.
—never fully dormant, never fully engaged.
And all the while this is what the sign around my neck said:
If it rattles like a person then it is a person.

III

negotiating fault lines . . .

ODE TO TIME, LANCE AND DECEMBER RAIN

Tonight's riotous rain has stirred in me
an impulse towards sacramental prayers
in the driveway, a chorus of hosannas,
a thousand novenas to the moon.

      Inside the deep pall of December—
      imagining the renewal of something
      called time—a rush of gratitude
      pulls at me like an undertow

of breaking currents, a crescendo
of applause to every unlikely image
that burns its reverse self
into memory and longing.

      I am inclined to take a bow
      to the mountains in the distance
      like torsos in repose, and to the clouds
      that lie down along their pale white hips.

To the duplicitous people in the city
below wearing their slap-dash smiles
and phoning-it-in like crazy,
and to the charcoal freeway

      of branches on the neighbor's broken elm,
      smudged against a blue-black slate
      of sky. I'll recite three Hail Mary's to all
      the world's sorrows that I cannot mend

and to the furnace in the basement
clattering its final death throes.
And to the two drenched boys
in red ties and overcoats

who knocked on our door last night;
I mistook them for the pizza delivery
guy and told them as much.
We shared a little chuckle, then I noticed

the taller one's name badge that said "Lance"
"The Church of Jesus Christ of Latter-Day Saints."
What are you two doing out
on a night like this? I asked.

Lance began to say something like
in snow and sleet and . . .
I smiled my best serene smile
and interrupted Lance with

Well, we're all full up here, but do carry on.
They smiled too and told me they hoped
my pizza got here soon. I watched
their thin-rounded shoulders

as they descended the stairs
and turned back into the down-pour
of night. What more saintly wish
could they have bestowed on me

than one of sustenance? Bless you boys—
may your latter days be absent of regret—
as unlikely as that will be.
May you say the wrong thing

        to someone you love and endure
        the hard lessons that follow.
        I'll write an ode to your fresh souls
        that walk around in your young bodies

and to your deep and natural
desire to believe in something
beyond those bodies. I wish
you heartbreak and hard work,

        debt, a dying furnace and a questioning
        that never ends. I wish you shock and disbelief
        when one of you hears of the other's death.
        May your latter days be a goddamn roller-coaster

of wonder and worn-out stupors, good sex
with the wrong person and just one insightful
moment of gratitude so intense
you burst out crying on a public bus.

        May you live a life that has you thanking
        any number of Gods that you are
        a sentient being well on your way
        to disappearing in December rain.

It's Like This

It may be that life is only worthwhile at moments.
Perhaps that is all we ought to expect.
—Sherwood Anderson

You're in the everydayness of it,
stuck in the human groove,
      the endless refrain.
It really is difficult
      to keep going—
what with the cats trying to speak,
      the daylilies dying
in full view of the kitchen window
and the half-hidden bed of dandelions
      that the mower missed.
It's like that with us—
      negotiating
fault lines
      between the miraculous
and the mundane.
How else could you do it?
      This daydream,
          this trick of the mind.
We can't all be Gurus
      of the Moment, Masters
      of the Now.
Better to join the mortal troop
      if only for the comfort
of a good grooming.
Nirvana must be

a lonely place.
Allow me
      my tribal nature, my pedestrian habits.
In all my lemmingness—
      let me be
one of *them*.

I (In the Absence of *You*—Meaning *Me*)

Don't talk to me
about upping the emotional ante.
If love were all that mattered
we wouldn't be having this conversation.
Consider the barefaced *I*—construct, artifice, caprice,
a notion to be played at. Like a troubled child I should stand
before the blackboard and write it a hundred times—*I, I, I* . . .
until it loses all meaning and falls to the ground like empty sound.
I might even forget how to spell it, simply refer to myself as *persona of naught,*
pronoun to the power of zilch. It's no accident that *eye* and *I* sound the same—
eye the vision, *I* the self (now there's a homophone you just gotta love.)
(And when I say *you* I mean *you* the reader.) So, here we are back at love again
(in this case *we* refers to the universal *we*, which of course includes *me*.)
That's all right, call it *love, instinct, need, self-preservation,*
but know it for what it is: a pretense to be named, the story of a story.
There are family photo's I have not looked at in years.
The same ones I pondered as a child, studied for hidden clues, the missed gesture,
the half open door behind someone's head. Here's the one of my mother and me
at the base of the ruins in Oaxaca, her hand on my shoulder, the sun
making us both squint. Here's the one of her yucking it up at her cousin's
wedding. So fully herself. So much a *self.*
—It takes years to see your life unfold
in chapters and if now is a chapter I'll look back on years hence and judge
like some tedious novel I nurtured too long, I'd like to think I did not hunger
for illumination too deeply or lie to myself too often or imbue too many hours
with hope. At the end of each day when nothing is touching my skin
but air, in that nightly ritual of disarmament, the physical *I* laid bare, I can't help
but desire one more step, just beyond the body. What release might be had

in shedding this noisy temporal reminder, with all its speeches and tirades, its many interr-
uptions. In the meantime, let's say that years from now, we
(yes, *you* and *me*) will look back on this conversation and roar with laughter over the empty sound of *I*.

As If

All maps did not lead here
       and the roof of the neighbor's house were not telling
       you something slanted, sideways, a fall to come, the edge, the lip,
       a slipping down.
As if this house were not your breath and pulse, its eaves and siding
       weighted to your skin and the appliances did not watch
       with suspicion, opening and closing with you
       every day in the same t-shirt, the same instructions to the cats.
As if you had a play to conclude,
       a comeuppance to render, an arrow to take.
As if all your life you thought you were headed *somewhere*
       and the wind outside did not admonish, battering the walls
       with its violent hoodoo, pushing you off-sync. Akimbo.
As if the truth were not eating its sandwich beside you every day
       and the voice from your head were not preferable to the voice
       from your throat.
As if *now* were not the point and you weren't missing it all
       in your absent-minded plotting. You have to wonder at all the things
       you do to say this is *mine*. See, I mopped the floor, washed the pan,
       inspected the oven for flaws, and that man who walks through the door
       every day recognizes you from the day before; he says *hi honey*
       as if he knew you.
As it is, you make believe—As if *this*. As if *that*.
       Time will pass, and you will be left
       with words fluttering in the air
       as if the night's corporeal box did not close
       and keep you still.

MOMENTARY MOTHER

At the public beach all afternoon, nothing unusual to report;
kids screaming into the waves, mothers shouting out warnings.
Americana has sprawled itself all over another Sunday.
When I see an African woman roll out her towel on the white sand.
Her orange Dashiki and yellow head-band flutter
like low-flying kites in the wind off the lake.
She sits herself down and waves
to her children already in the water. Meanwhile,
a three-year-old blonde beauty in mini-bikini
with shovel and bucket sits herself within inches of the woman
and begins the serious business of piling sand.
The woman regards the child—smiles
and in one fluid instinctual motion
reaches out to straighten the child's bathing suit,
brushes off a bit of sand from the girl's shoulder,
leans back and looks out at her own children
treading and splashing. The girl does not react.
She does not register the gesture at all, but continues
to shovel and fill. And why not?
Here there is sand and water
and the beach is teeming with mothers.

FOR A SINGLE SUMMER

or winter retreat, I'd like someone else
to tend to my fears. Here, I want to say,

to my neighbor Walter, just keep them in a box
in the basement till I get back.

They don't eat much, mostly each other.
They keep their own company.

No need to mist their roots or talk to them
at night. They are nothing

if not healthy. I'll be at the beach
or a cabin in the woods. I'll be on Venus

taking the waters, floating lovely
in my gossamer gown. I'll be asleep

for ten thousand years. I'll take no
calls and never bathe.

Light and air will fill my body.
My mind will grow

moss. I will think
white thoughts.

Here's my husband's number,
though he can't take them either.

He has too many of his own as it is.
We spent years shoving our particular boxes

back and forth across the kitchen table,
scratching the Formica and damning each other.

He would try to stab mine with male guilt
and I practically loved his to death.

In time we fashioned them
into complicated centerpieces

and stationed them above the fireplace.
But after years of walking past them

they lost their appeal, required too much
dusting and explanations to guests.

We finally packed them away, stifled their muffled protest
under excelsior and hoped they died a nun's death.

FACING THE RAIN

It was cats and dogs this morning,
pelting my thin coat and thinner resolve
as I wandered past mounds of winter harvest;
purple kohlrabi, kale and carrots
stacked together in tri-colored pyramids.
The convivial voices of vendors echoed
through the canyon of brick store fronts
and provisional pop-up shelters. The under-fur
of small dogs dragged in the puddles
            at my feet.
Now, hours later, lying back with a book
and a mind full of quandary, the sun
has made its way through and is casting shadows
off the bean tree in the front yard.
The black relief of leaves flicker
against the window's slatted blinds.
Though the cats are asleep in a heap
under the leather chair, a mass
of rising and ascending amiability,—
            all is never *all-well*—
I am thrown in the tailspin
of mourning the moment I am in
while I am in it, constant negotiations
with the now and the eternal
drawing of new cards. I am forever gesturing
at the proverbial dealer across the table
with a kind of gimme motion from an up-turned hand
—*hit me*, I tell him, that's the term I'm looking for—*hit me*.
Give it to me straight, I can take it.

Render me luckless and loony . . . *call me
irresponsible*, but grant me a do-over, another chance
at randomness . . . I'm game, I'm ready.
I'm facing the rain, and not giving in.

After

After his wife had left him
in that oh so final way,
we brought our friend and his daughter food.
The news had come as a sudden blow
so I grabbed what we had; the loaf of bread
bought for dinner, cans of tuna saved for lunch.
Standing in his doorway, unshaven, looking
decades older than he had the day before—
he received these gifts like lost children,
gathered them into his arms and held them to his chest.
Following him to the kitchen we found every visible surface
covered with food; tin-foil topped pie plates, plastic bowls of soup,
glass jars of spaghetti sauce, loaf after loaf of bread.
He shook his head and said *well, we certainly won't go hungry.*
No, I thought, you won't. It's the most that we can do—
to offer your bodies substance. To come and go.
To say eat this and live.

CHECKOUT LINE

In that long receding
I read a few poems and iced my thoughts;
causeway to some private nomenclature
and the coil I cannot shuffle off.

I read a few poems and iced my thoughts,
alone in the elysian field of memory
and the coil I cannot shuffle off.
Clutching my bonus points, alone

in the elysian fields of memory,
dreading the load speakers
and clutching my bonus points.
I bivouacked through a ©Habitrail of desire.

And in that long receding
I composed a requiem for all the other shoppers,
bivouacking their way through a ©Habitrail of desire
and the coil they cannot shuffle off.

THE MASS MIGRATION OF 60 MILLION MONARCH BUTTERFLIES MAY SOON BE HISTORY

No, I will not sign your petition because I am full of the drama of being me and my heart has four chambers to fill and release, even in this morning of self-doubt, with its clouds of appeasement and a thousand dreary little flowers. I know Monsanto is evil incarnate, but like most things in this world they are bigger than me and my arms resemble wet flypaper from fighting all the things in this world that are bigger than me. I can barely flip an egg or write this poem. Besides, I have always been jealous of butterflies, with their runway worthy wardrobes and their ability to lift themselves into flight whenever the conversation becomes trite. I cannot contribute to the redemption of the world right now—my father has dementia, my husband is almost out of breath-right-strips and the cat barfed in the hallway, again. Today in the kitchen of no-sympathy I tried to hack away at the dry-rot of remorse, but my ego of no-return had gone on a sabbatical of never-ending proof. At this very moment, my heart may be choking on its own fumes. Plus, next December I'll be fifty and I haven't even been to France.

Can butterflies surmise their own demise? My mother had a butterfly tattoo on her right shoulder. It was brightly colored at first (as most things were in the 1970's) but over the years it faded to a muddled black outline of something that might have resembled a butterfly at one time. One of her favorite movies was *Papillon* which means butterfly in French, but she was Spanish. She said *Ay, Dios Mio* a lot and made us go to midnight mass. What is this nostalgia that comes with autumn? This power-mower of want? Can I get a witness? Can I get validation? Can I lie down, right here, in the shadow of your verdict? This morning the tulips' first green leaves in the muddy yard appeared, after twenty-three straight days of rain. Persistent protesters; I forget about them mostly. Yes, I know that radioactive fertilizer is the surprising primary cause of lung cancer in smokers, but I am concerned about the spider that lives in our mailbox, the implied havoc of the hose and the hobgoblins that stomp around the red habitat of my erratic heart, the one that has been beating nonstop for forty-nine years. Think about that—forty-nine years of nonstop beating.

You want me to think about mining and drilling on public lands during the government shutdown? I will try, but frankly I'd rather consider the watermelon radish and its similarity to an exploding star, a dying planet of sharp and peppery, sweet and bitter overtones. A virtual umami party slivered into cross-sections and tiled onto the greeny roof of my salad. It's a lot like chaos theory, in which something ever so small (like the beating of butterfly wings) results in something huge, like the formation of a hurricane or the creation of a universe. This is called The Butterfly Effect. Isn't that how it goes? You think something small and beautiful only applies to the moment, its impact fleeting and somehow insignificant. I do feel guilty that I don't live in the first state to require GMO labeling, but then I generally live in a state of indecision. I am sorry that Wall Street is seeking last minute loopholes, but aren't we all? Couldn't everyone use a really good loophole, especially at the last minute? Considering how, along with the Monarch Butterfly, we will all, soon enough, be history.

It's Always Something

The aspen doing something in the wind
—Robert Hass

This dream again,

where I wander deep halls

in the museum of lost meaning

and the saints are busy conferring about something

in the della Francesca.

A resurrection of cranes

stood aloof and rigid, a black-eyed junco half-way off the frame.

Even the magpies seem to have been struck dumb.

While an approximation of angels held the silent O of their lips

and looked toward heaven—the notion of God doing something

to their souls.

Is there a word for all the unsayable confines of the world?

Something beyond conformity, just this side of dismissal?

As the undercurrent of years

does *something*

to your life. All those hours

spent comparing

one beauty to another, whether on the canvas or beyond the gallery doors—

the moon doing something in the sky.

WHAT GOES AROUND

It's not like I entered
    the moon's orbit.
Not like I discovered cricket science
    or mouse culture.
It's only that vestibule called the mind—echo chamber,
    kiosk of chaos, cone of delusion—no escaping
this shaky barrier
    of bones, though relief
efforts are under way.
If I am not reading the scrim
    of the water's surface
than I am telling fortunes in the alley, divining
    my demise.
Look—I am a body, a brain, bag-o'-bits,
    a ruse, redolent
with worry, bursting, near doom.
Think of the widow who ordered a staircase built
    to a brick wall, the child who spins
solely for the purpose of falling. I too made myself
    redundant, superfluous.
    Wasn't it always so?
The black stone carried back
from the *Mediterranean*—proof—a solid piece
    of evidential matter—*I convey,*
    therefore I am.
Woe all these digressions, the many-colored attempts
at evasion; this is my thicket,
    my muddle,
    my quagmire.

From the breach of morning
      light to the dispelled night—
I watch the trillium grow,
occupy my head
      with makeshift metaphors
and these three stations
      of the cross: reverie, what if
and the frozen tundra of now.

A Day in the Life

It is 8 a.m. and everyone is waiting
for their lives to begin. We have made it
through the bad machinery of night
and await the conundrum of another day.

With backpacks and satchels full
of hypnotic computations, we walk
like accidental anthems with hands
in pockets to bus stop and office,

our usual seat behind the podium,
where some small manifesto
of self emerges, another way
to proclaim our aim, reiteration

of mandate and mantra.
Soon it is 12 p.m. and the clock
has cut the day in half.
Now a respite from the morning

grind, now a downhill slide. Before we know it
it is 4 p.m. and everyone is waiting
for the day to end. With a slowing of the breath
and a cooling of the skin, every gesture a rendered amen;

the pen laid down, the phone ignored,
each chair rolled neatly to its given slot.
With eyes firming in their gaze and a gait
adjusting to the evening routine—

we have carried ourselves well,
contained the troublesome boundaries
of the body and surrendered,
yet again, to a rendition of one.

THE END IS NEAR

No kidding, and let me guess,
it's later than I think?
Like I don't know that.
Like I can't see
the reciprocity of nature
in all its beginnings and endings,—
be it Buddhist or otherwise—
Like I didn't notice the 13th century
Duomo in the piazza, the bell tower,
the cobble stone dust whirling
towards my face. Like I couldn't tell you
that I am not exactly young
anymore, neither am I old. I will not be swept away
from parties to the barn. No more kissing
impromptu with you and you and you.
Last night, a woman in a movie,
learning that her father might die (sooner than later),
said, *I can handle the fact that he'll die. I just can't handle*
that it will be forever. I laughed out loud
and then burst into tears. I'd like to stop
weighing my options
as if I were the embodiment of discreet mathematics.
I'd like to stop sitting on the banks of the river Ganges,
half blind, attempting to solve the unknowns. I'd like to stop
appreciating my condition. Never mind—reprise the reprise.
Name your children after mystics if it makes you feel better.
Call it Belladonna or Deadly Nightshade—
the plant remains the same. We can't help craving
euphemisms. It's like Rome, only more familiar.

FRIDAY

And I am losing language.
Taken with the strange
geography of the body. Agog.
The lay of the land so prescient
and movable, so pliant and usable.
(Something about the body and how you walk
around in it. How all the elements called *you*
are transported from bed to sink, pavement to car.)
How did I become my own beast-
of-burden? Carbon based, fuel hungry—
Automatic Response System?
Rapt. Practically spellbound
by all the gestures of modern life
dictated by circumstance; place hand here, wrap fingers
around shaft of spoon, rotate in a circular motion.
A congress of one, I am both audience and actor,
writer and reader. Egging myself on—I laugh
at all the right moments, shake my head in disbelief
at the predictable dialog and tired scenarios.
Look—a hand, an eye, the profile of a face.
Given the inability to see
inward, I hover above
my own topography. Barely attaining
an aerial view—bee to my buzz, prop-
plane to landing strip, satellite to planet.
And all the while this is what the sign on my back said;
Applause now. House lights down. Exit stage left.

BIOGRAPHICAL NOTE

Photo Credit: Melinda Cogen

Tina Schumann is a pushcart nominated poet and the author of three poetry collections, *As If* (Parlor City Press, 2010) which was awarded the Stephen Dunn Poetry Prize, *Requiem. A Patrimony of Fugues* (Diode Editions, 2016) which won the Diode Editions Chapbook Contest for 2016, and *Praising the Paradox* (Red Hen Press, 2019) which was a finalist in the National Poetry Series, Four Way Books Intro Prize and the New Issues Poetry Prize. She is editor of the IPPY award-winning anthology *Two-Countries. U.S. Daughters and Sons of Immigrant Parents* (Red Hen Press, 2017). Her work received the 2009 American Poet Prize from *The American Poetry Journal*, finalist status in the Terrain.org annual poetry contest, as well as honorable mention in *The Atlantic*. She is a poetry editor with Wandering Aengus Press and Assistant Director at Artsmith.org. Her poems have appeared in publications and anthologies since 1999 including *The American Journal of Poetry*, *Ascent, Crab Creek Review, Cimarron Review, Michigan Quarterly Review, Nimrod, Parabola, Palabra, Poetry International, The Yale Journal for Humanities in Medicine* and *Verse Daily*. You can read more about Tina at www.tinaschumann.com.